THE JORDAN PETERSON CHEAT SHEET

"Pursue what is meaningful, not what is expedient"

A collection of Jordan Peterson quotes and images for coloring

A Prelude...

"That's another hallmark of truth, is that it snaps things together. People write to me all the time and say it's as if things were coming together in my mind. It's like the Platonic idea that all learning was remembering. You have a nature, and when you feel that nature articulated, it's like the act of snapping the puzzle pieces together. "
Jordan Peterson

Coloring & the Map of Meaning

Why would a person spend time coloring? Remember a few years ago? Sales in adult coloring books went through the roof! Studies subsequently have shown that coloring has therapeutic effects. The trend may have cooled down but I'm going to suggest that important truths are embedded in the act of coloring and that this medium is an untapped teaching tool. We have what to learn and master, psychologically speaking, if we will take on this discipline. Further, coloring books can teach content, specifically ideas from the realm of psychology, important lessons about self, life, identity and more.

I invite you on a path of self-exploration. We are taking a bit of a tour into some of the ideas that Dr. Jordan Peterson has put forward, ideas that are helping some make very interesting changes in their lives. Welcome to the coloring book for 'lobsters', the term that Peterson enthusiasts use to describe themselves. Now let's get a bit of an introduction to his ideas.

Learning How to See

In different ways, we are fooled by reality. By way of example, we are naive to the nuance in everyday things. We rush around and lose awareness, say, of the magnificently intricate patterns in nature. Take the following example: you look up, averting your eyes from the computer, and catch a glimpse of the tree outside. You see 'tree'. You don't process the collage of leaves, layers of texture, the color palettes. You just see 'tree'.

Many adult coloring books bring awareness to the complex repeating patterns in the world around us. These books often emphasize and exaggerate detail. Gertrude Stein said: " I like to go to museums. I like to go to museums so I can look out the window." Coloring books, similarly, let us 'look out the window'.

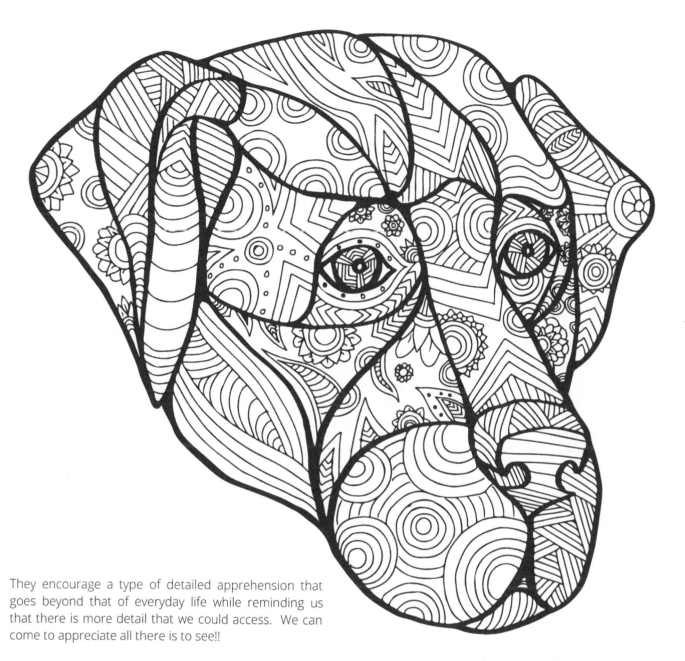

They encourage a type of detailed apprehension that goes beyond that of everyday life while reminding us that there is more detail that we could access. We can come to appreciate all there is to see!!

Now there's another way we are fooled by reality. Your perceptual systems represent the world as coherent and organized. You recognize the objects around you, the people, the sounds. Is reality really that orderly, though? It isn't. You are only perceiving a thin band of the present.

You sit under a tree at the nearby park. Say you're in a quiet, contemplative mood. The weather is pleasant. The view is peaceful. There is this quality of stillness although you are aware of background sounds. Are you fully registering the reality of the moment? What aren't you seeing?

You're not seeing the buzz of insects that are ensconced in their busyness right near you. If children are playing in the distance, you hear them but you're not seeing the actual soundwaves which carry the sounds. For that matter, you're not seeing other waves that are similarly invisible to the human eye. You know that in the homes nearby there are televisions, telephones, radios, computers, all receiving data. If you could consciously perceive the various frequencies streaming above you and around you, the scene would probably be quite busy. My point here is that reality, in reality, is complex, multi-faceted and chaotic. We are spared a good deal of information.

Some adult coloring books bring us to a realization about reality. They remind us that we live amidst infinite detail and complexity. They emphasize that complexity, requiring us to commune with it, versus tune it out.

Along those lines, coloring books require us to patiently invest in an activity that requires fidelity to detail. The activity pays off to the degree that you focus single-mindedly on each small segment. The activity and its impressive product when it is well done, is a lesson we can easily generalize to life itself. "Imagine if I put that much intention, care and follow-through on all my activities!" How many of your outcomes would be that much better, if you did everything to the standard that you use when working on an adult coloring book?

We are going to see that working with a coloring book will help deliver content that relates to the self as it processes a complex reality and simultaneously offers a process that, itself, is both instructive and therapeutic. I think you will also see that there is another layer of learning and reflection that occurs when we think about ideas and process them using visual media. Visual images give us another way of unpacking the ideas.

Further, thinking about quotes shared by Dr. Jordan Peterson, we are going to learn about reality, about order and chaos, about the self and the challenges of bringing that self to fruition. But first, you might want to grab some gel pens and get to work!

Order & Chaos

One page back we see a picture of buildings. On one hand, there's something compelling about the arrangement, the variability, the multiplicity. There is the cityscape, the vastness of it, the busyness. And then we imagine life inside all these units. Imagine the chaos! Imagine the busyness! As if there is life teeming within, such complexity.

In reality, the landscape is characterized by objects and empty space. Streets and driveways are empty, allowing their use. The ordered design facilitates city life. In that image meant to be colored we get a more intense representation. Buildings crammed together leaves an impression of chaos. With the way coloring books often render reality so that detail prevails, it leads to thoughts about chaos and order, taking me to ideas advanced by Jordan Peterson. Peterson makes the following point: all of reality is characterized by a chaotic complexity and, bit by bit, our task is to chew off little bits of the chaos, organize those bits, and master them.

We start this project when we are infants. Initially, the world is a blur of sounds, colors and shadows. A baby's eyes will not focus. The child's experience is impressionistic. It will take time before the baby is able to interpret depth of field, able to understand patterns and attach them to different people or objects. Until that occurs, the environment is awash with complexity.

With time, that baby will make discernments. recognizing facial features as those of specific people, etc. Gradually, the perceptual apparatus develops and the baby awakens to an order that he or she is now able to perceive. The environment becomes more predictable and easier to understand.

Once the child masters the home environment, though, it's time to to move on to 'higher order' chaos. For example, at a certain point it's time to become familiar with these black shapes that we call letters and numbers. It will take some time until the child is able to interpret them and read them. Coming upon those letters and numbers, playing with toys that showcase those forms, will be the first encounter with these strange symbols. Then looking at books, gibberish that makes no sense. Then starting to sound out letters. And so on, and so forth. Gradually chaos becomes order. Now it's time to go to school and confront more bits of reality that have been, hitherto, unexplored.

We will see that all of life can be reduced to this task: figuring out aspects of reality that are unfamiliar, whether that looks like studying biology or algebra, whether it means getting behind the wheel of a car and learning how to drive. At the outset, every domain we take on is the new chaos that we are going to master. Gradually, we learn how to relate to this corner of the universe. We learn how to use Excel. We take up a new hobby or learn a new language. We take music lessons. So it goes, And gradually, we are turning chaos into habitable order, all

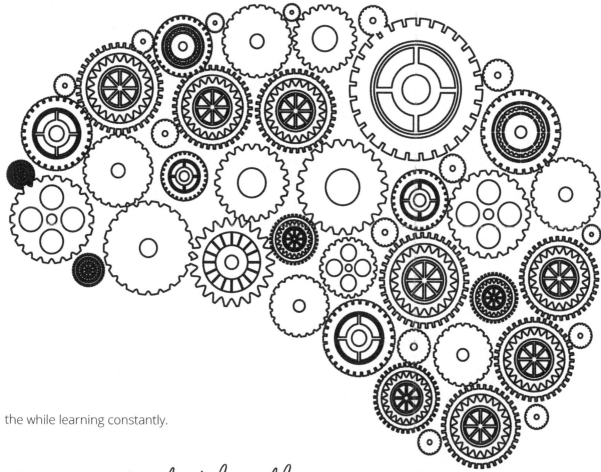

the while learning constantly.

Processing a Complicated World

Because there are always aspects of reality that are new and unfamiliar, we have to come up with generalizations at a very young age which we can apply, lest we be flummoxed by new situations. Peterson points out that we will podge together a map of sorts when we are very young. It is a map that we harbor in the unconscious mind, a map we use very actively *without knowing that we are doing so*! How does that work?

Say you are a child and, over time, you have formed impressions of adults, of boys, of girls based on the people you know already. You've filed away your impressions of what adults, boys or girls are like (each in their own category) and have come up with what you think you can reasonably expect from people in each of these categories. The beliefs and expectations you come up with are not consciously held ideas, mind you. You harbor these ideas quietly in the unconscious. Next time you meet an adult, a boy or a girl, those learnings guide you. They influence how you will behave with new people, how you will interpret their behaviors.

If the beliefs and expectations you filed away are accurate and reasonable, you will be in good shape. You will wind up behaving in a way that will be well received and your dealings will be successful. If you managed to acquire learnings that, unfortunately, were inaccurate, your dealings may not be successful. You will be frustrated by negative outcomes and you will feel confused: "What happened? Why didn't that work out?"

What's an example? Imagine a kid comes from a very informal home. The habit in that home is to dry hands after bathroom use with anything that remotely looks like a towel. This kid visits a friend's house and, after washing hands, reaches for a hanging terrycloth robe to dry the hands. If the family members from that home observe that use, perhaps they will be upset. One family teaches one norm, another advances another! That's just one simple example of how the map we come up with may include lessons or learnings that are not universal truths! There may be social repercussions, or functional repercussions when harboring ideas which conflict with the map of other people!

harbored in the unconscious mind, *we don't even realize we are using a map*! We think we are perceiving reality and acting in a way that is reasonable and objective..

You would think that if we are applying principles or ideas that are out of date, that we would figure it out quickly. Let's remember a line coined by Albert Einstein. Einstein said, " Believing is seeing!" Once you get a notion in your head, the truth of it seems indisputable! Often people only see that which confirms what they already believe! In psychology, this tendency is called 'confirmation bias'. People see or notice only what they expect to see. Why? Because seeing something that opposes their beliefs is destabilizing, making people doubt themselves on a number of levels. People, therefore, prefer certainty and look to justify what they already believe.

The map a person puts together at a young age includes rules about how to behave, guesses about what could reasonably be expected from other people, also visions of what is valuable, outcomes to be pursued, and what is to be avoided at all costs. Let's think about this map as resembling the Pirates map, a map that shows where the gold is and what

Rules to the Rescue!

We have these maps. Our maps harbor errors and faulty learnings. We will do better if we update our maps. What should we do?

Psychologist Jordan Peterson would tell you to study learnings and rules for life which are tried and true. In fact, Peterson himself has written books and made lectures available on YouTube which advance just these sorts of rules and learnings. Many have been able to use his insights to achieve monumental life changes.

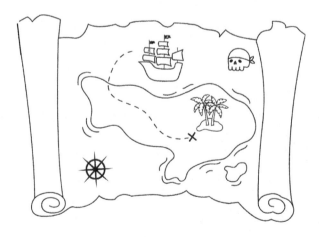

route to take to find it. And we need to remember, the map might not be that accurate. It might be partly accurate. It might be highly flawed. After all, we cobbled together this map, the first working draft, when we were five years old. We shouldn't be shocked if the rules or beliefs we adopted as kids turn out to be flagrantly wrong. And, of course, the whole issue is extra tricky because if the map is

In this coloring book, then, I'd like to introduce some of the rules or principles that he has advanced, sharing some quotes that have served as guidance for many. Coloring the images that help animate the ideas gives you an opportunity to 'marinate' in any given teaching. Concentrate on what your life would look like if you integrated any of these ideas into your playbook/map of meaning. Make the changes and you can achieve some new outcomes while simultaneously updating the map you harbor in the unconscious mind. Don't be surprised if the next step has you wandering over to YouTube to listen to the lectures that have changed the landscape of life, for many, many people. Strongly recommending!

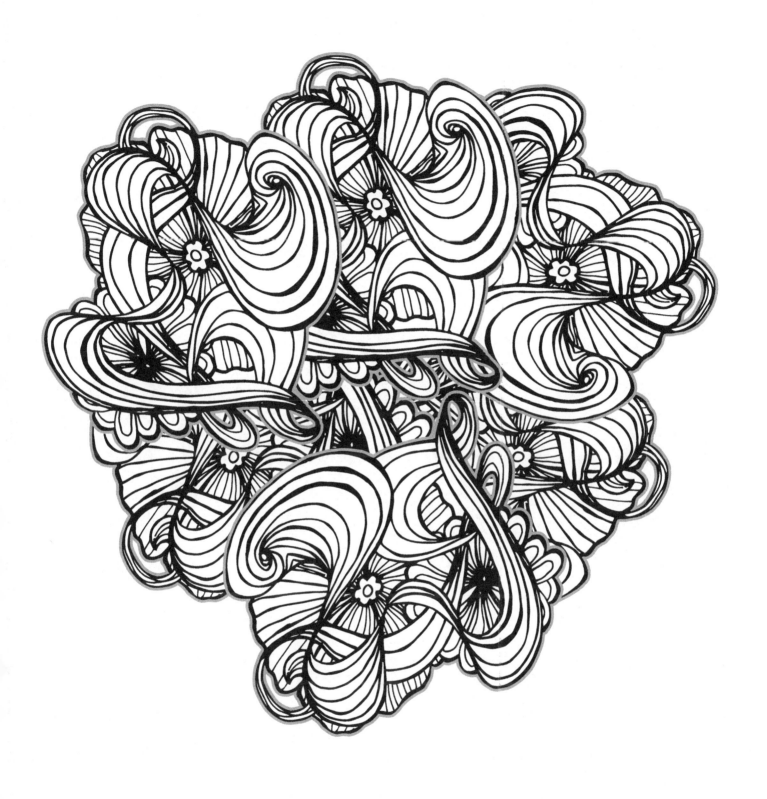

The Chaos in Life!

The Rules

"There is no shortage of wisdom and guidance outside of us, embedded in the social world. Why rely on our own limited resources to remember the road, or to orient ourselves a new territory, when we can rely on signs and guideposts placed there so effortfully by others?"

Jordan Peterson, *Beyond Order: 12 More Rules for Life*

"So, attend carefully to your posture. Quit drooping and hunching around. Speak your mind. Put your desires forward, as if you had a right to them – at least the same right as others. Walk tall and gaze forthrightly ahead. Dare to be dangerous. Encourage the serotonin to flow plentifully through the neural pathways desperate for its calming influence."

"Aggression underlies the drive to be outstanding, to be unstoppable, to compete, to win – to be actively virtuous, at least along one dimension. Determination is its admirable pro-social face."

Jordan Peterson

"You must determine where you are going in your life, because you cannot get there unless you move in that direction. Random wandering will not move you forward. It will instead disappoint and frustrate you and make you anxious and unhappy and hard to get along with, and then resentful, and then vengeful, and then worse."
Jordan Peterson

Yesterday

"Compare yourself to who you were yesterday, not who somebody else is today."

Today

"Obviously I'm not perfect but I'm slightly less terrible than I was yesterday. You keep that up for five years and you're wherever you should be."
Jordan Peterson

"If you will not reveal yourself to others, you cannot reveal yourself to yourself. That does not only mean that you suppress who you are, although it also means that. It means that so much of what you could be will never be forced by necessity to come forward."
Jordan Peterson

"Pursue what is meaningful (not what is expedient)."
Jordan Peterson

"Pet a cat
when you see one
on the street."
Jordan Peterson

"The way that you make people resilient is by voluntarily exposing them to things that they are afraid of and that makes them uncomfortable."
Jordan Peterson

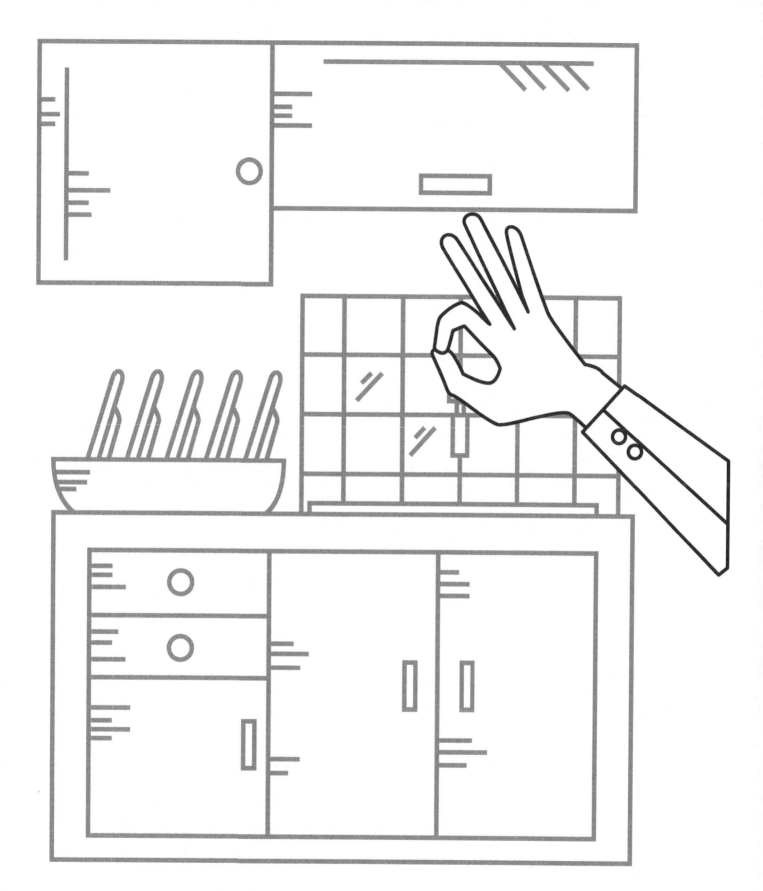

"Set your house in perfect order
before you criticize the world."
Jordan Peterson

"You cannot be protected from the things that frighten you and hurt you, but if you identify with the part of your being that is responsible for transformation, then you are always the equal, or more than the equal of the things that frighten you."
Jordan Peterson

"You have to treat yourself like you matter because if you don't then you don't take care of yourself and you become vengeful and cruel and you take it out on people around you and you are not a positive force. None of that is good...you suffer more and so does everyone else around you."
Jordan Peterson

"It took untold generations to get you where you are.
A little gratitude might be in order."
Jordan Peterson

"Our eyes are always pointing at things we are interested in approaching, or investigating, or looking for, or having. We must see, but to see, we must aim, so we are always aiming."

Jordan Peterson

"What is your friend: the things you know, or the things you don't know. First of all, there's a lot more things you don't know. And second, the things you don't know is the birthplace of all your new knowledge! So, if you make the things you don't know your friend, rather than the things you know, well then you're always on a quest in a sense. You're always looking for new information in the off chance that somebody who doesn't agree with you will tell you something you couldn't have figured out on your own! It's a completely different way of looking at the world. It's the antithesis of opinionated."
Jordan Peterson

"Be the hero your mom wanted you to be."
Jordan Peterson

"Can you imagine yourself in 10 years if instead of avoiding the things you know you should do, you actually did them every single day. That's powerful."
Jordan Peterson

"Make friends with people who want the best for you."
Jordan Peterson

"**Do not hide unwanted things in the fog.**"
Jordan Peterson.

"Don't bother children when they are skateboarding."
Jordan Peterson

"Strengthen the individual. Start with yourself. Take care of yourself. Define who you are. Refine your personality. Choose your destination"

Jordan Peterson

"We cannot navigate, without something to aim at and, while we are in this world, we must always navigate."
Jordan Peterson

"You are morally obliged to take care of yourself. You should take care of, help and be good to yourself the same way you would take care of, help and be good to someone you loved and valued."

Jordan Peterson

"It is my firm belief that the best way to fix the world—a handyman's dream, if ever there was one—is to fix yourself,"
Jordan B. Peterson

"Don't fall in love with the worst of you."
Jordan Peterson"

"The secret to your existence is right in front of you,
and it manifests itself as all those things you know you
should do but you're avoiding."
Jordan Peterson

"The purpose of life is finding
the largest burden that you
can bear and bearing it."
Jordan Peterson

"Read something written by someone great."
Jordan Peterson

"Work as hard as you possibly can on at least one thing and see what happens."
Jordan Peterson

"Confront the chaos of Being. Take aim against a sea of troubles. Specify your destination, and chart your course."
Jordan Peterson

"Specify your damn goals
because how are you going to hit something
if you don't know what it is?"
Jordan Peterson

"Instead of protesting and trying to change the world, first win the war of evil within yourself. To make the world a better place first do the things you have to do everyday. And do them
- actually do them everyday."

Jordan Peterson

"Each individual has ultimate responsibility to bear;
that if one wants to live a full life, one first sets one's
own house in order; and only then can one sensibly
aim to take on bigger responsibilities."
Jordan Peterson

"Transform the chaos of potential into the realities of habitable order."
Jordan Peterson

"500 small decisions, 500 tiny actions, compose
your day, today, and every day. Could you aim
one or two of these at a better result?"
Jordan Peterson

"The Ideal"

"Don't kill your future self."
Jordan Peterson

"There are great ancestral figures nested within you.
Inside the darkest place is the heroic ancestor whose identity
you could incorporate."

Jordan Peterson

"What path are you on? Some of you is dark and some of you is light. . .get rid of the darkness and then you're on the path of light. What will happen to you when you're on the path of light? The best that can happen to you."
Jordan Peterson

"Anything you let win the internal argument grows. And anything you let be defeated shrinks."
Jordan Petterson

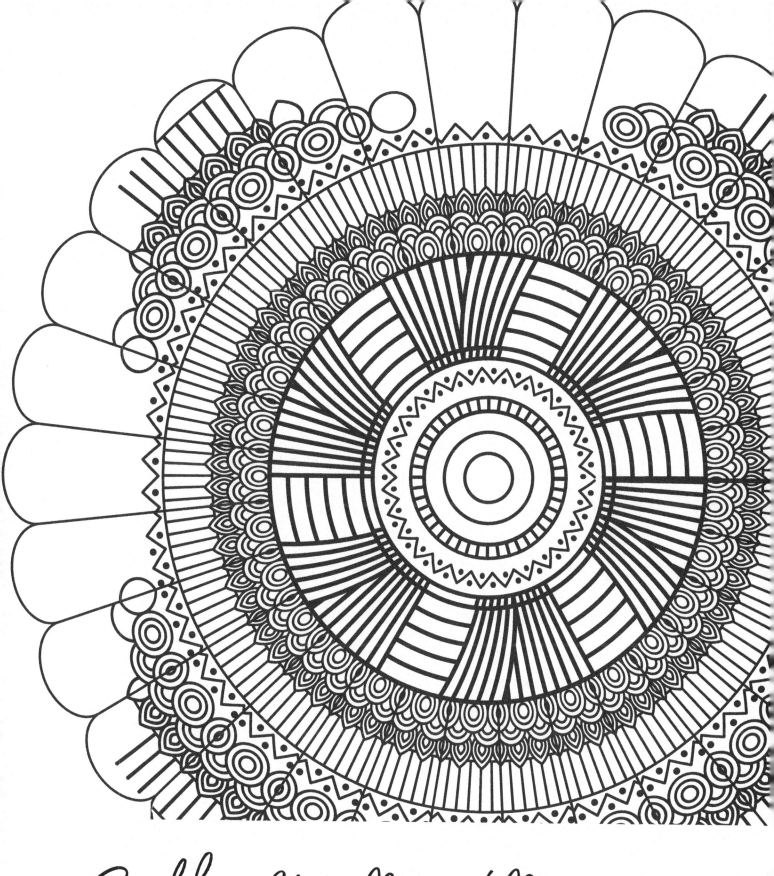

Building Your Map of Meaning

(More Jordan Peterson insights)

"Sometimes, when things are not going well, it's not the world that's the cause."
Jordan Peterson

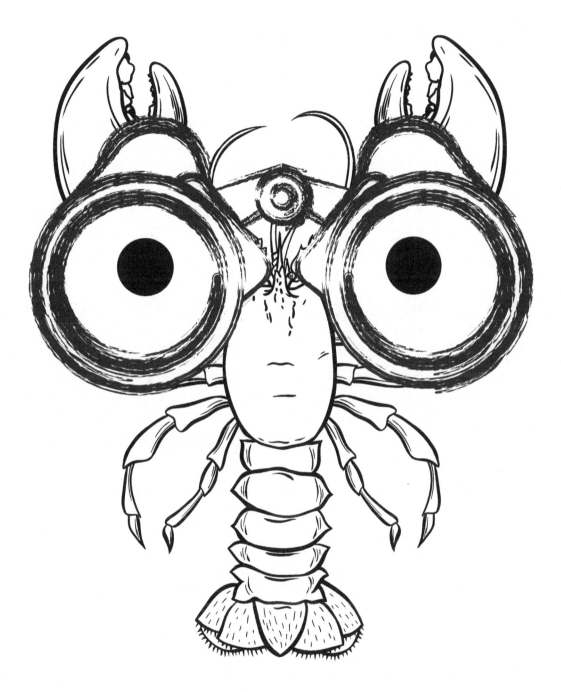

"Don't underestimate the power of vision and direction. These are irresistible forces, able to transform what might appear to be unconquerable obstacles into traversable pathways And expanding opportunities."
Jordan Peterson.

"If your life isn't going well,
perhaps it is your current knowledge
that is insufficient, not life itself."
Jordan Peterson

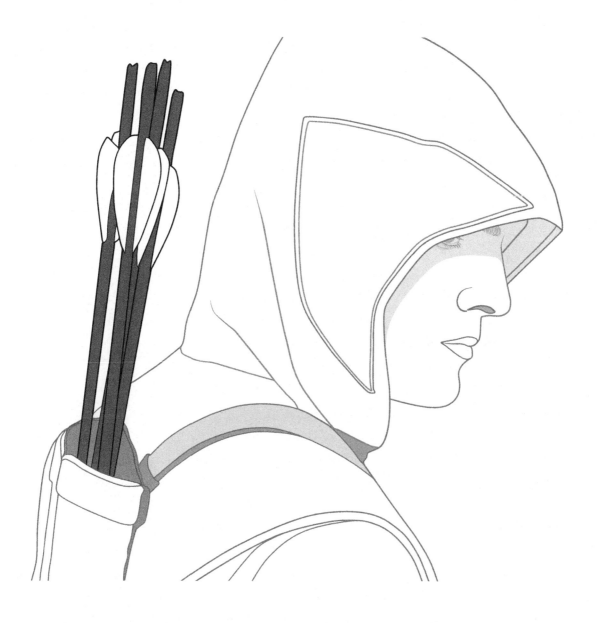

"Everybody acts out a myth, but very few people know what their myth is and you should know what your myth is, because it might be a tragedy. And maybe you don't want it to be."
— Jordan B. Peterson, The Psychological Significance of the Bible:

You could watch the precious days tick by. Or you could learn how to entice yourself into sustainable, productive activity. Do you ask yourself what you want? Do you negotiate fairly with yourself? Or are you a tyrant, with yourself as slave"

"It is not virtuous to be victimized by a bully, even if that bully is one self."
Jordan Peterson

"It's more difficult to rule yourself
than to rule your city."
Jordan Peterson

"As the situation degenerates, people have to be offered stupid amusements,
more frequently, for them to ignore what's actually going on."
Jordan Peterson

" If a man knows more than others,
he becomes lonely."
Carl Jung

"Dreams shed light on the dim places
where reason itself has yet to voyage."
Jordan Peterson

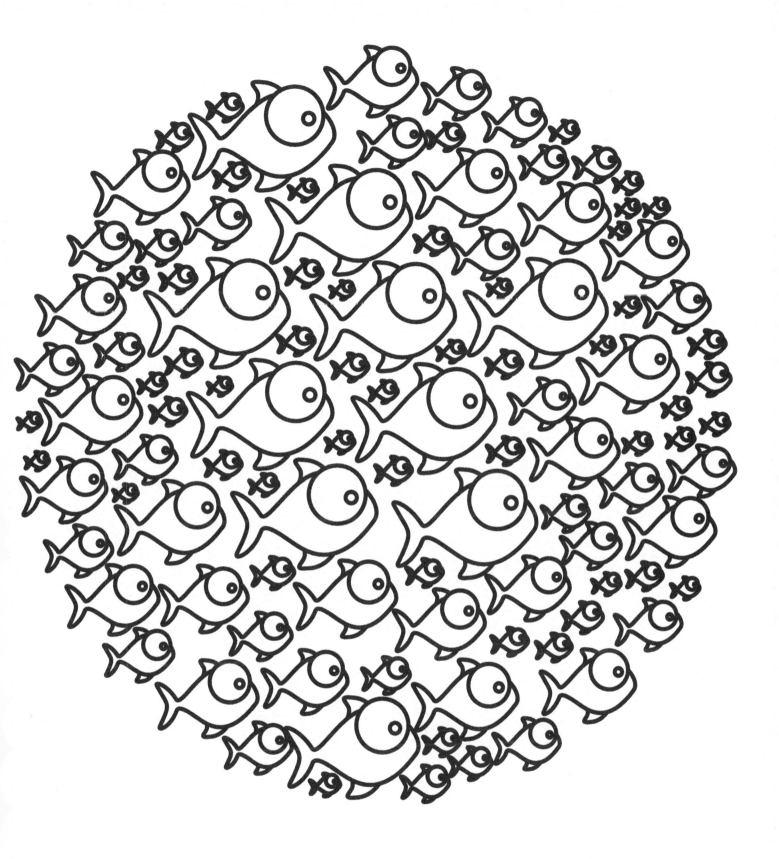

"It's not just human nature to associate in tribes.
It's deeper than that."
Jordan Peterson

"Always place your becoming above your current being."
Jordan Peterson

"You are a loose unity of a multiplicity of spirits many of which are doing their own thing and you are striving to bring them all to some form of unity."
Jordan Peterson

From *The Jordan Peterson Cheat Sheet: The Coloring Book that Will Change Your Life* by Annette Poizner, MSW, Ed.D., RSW

"You're going to pay a price for every bloody thing you do and everything you don't do. You don't get to choose to not pay a price. You get to choose which poison you're going to take. That's it."
Jordan Peterson

"It is not for nothing that our age cries out for the Redeemer personality, for the one who can emancipate himself from the grip of the collective psychosis & save at least his own soul, who lights a beacon of hope for others, proclaiming that here is at least one man who has succeeded in extricating himself from the fatal identity with the group psyche."
Carl Jung

"We are not equal in ability or outcome, and never will be. A very small number of people produce very much of everything. The winners don't take all, but they take most, and the bottom is not a good place to be."
Jordan Peterson

"If you have a comprehensive explanation for everything, then it decreases uncertainty and anxiety and reduces your cognitive load. And if you can use that simplifying algorithm to put yourself on the side of moral virtue then you're constantly a good person with a minimum of effort."

Jordan Peterson

"Because there are a lot of serious matters being discussed in the culture, at large, right now, it would be really good if everybody could keep their sense of humor. As long as we can keep a sense of humor, we are not as close to disaster as we might be."
Jordan Peterson

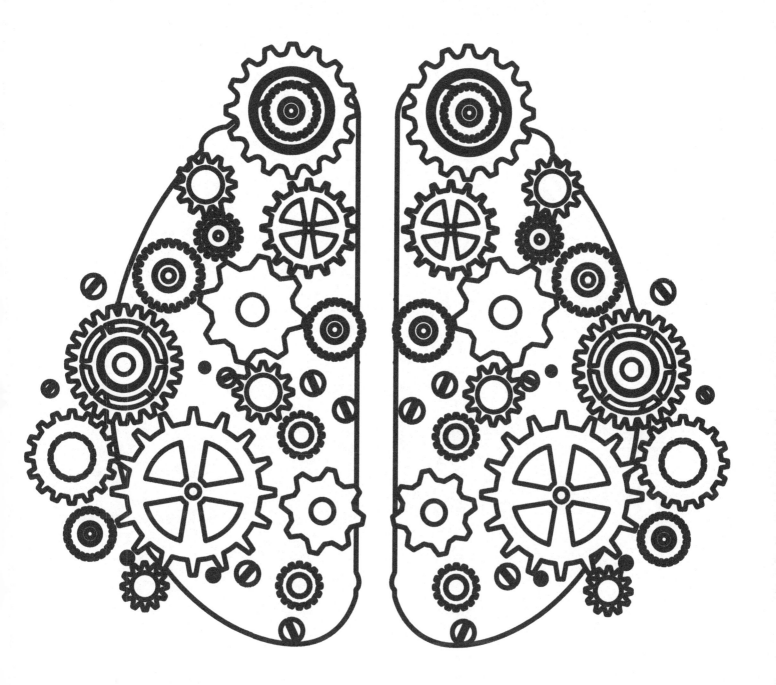

"Like Satan is the highest angel in G-d's heavenly kingdom, the intellect is the most powerful sub-element of the psyche. It's the thing that shines out above all within humanity, perhaps across the domain of life, itself. But it has a flaw: its flaw is that it falls in love with its own productions and assumes that they are total."
Jordan Peterson

"Your character is your mode to force forward."
Jordan Peterson

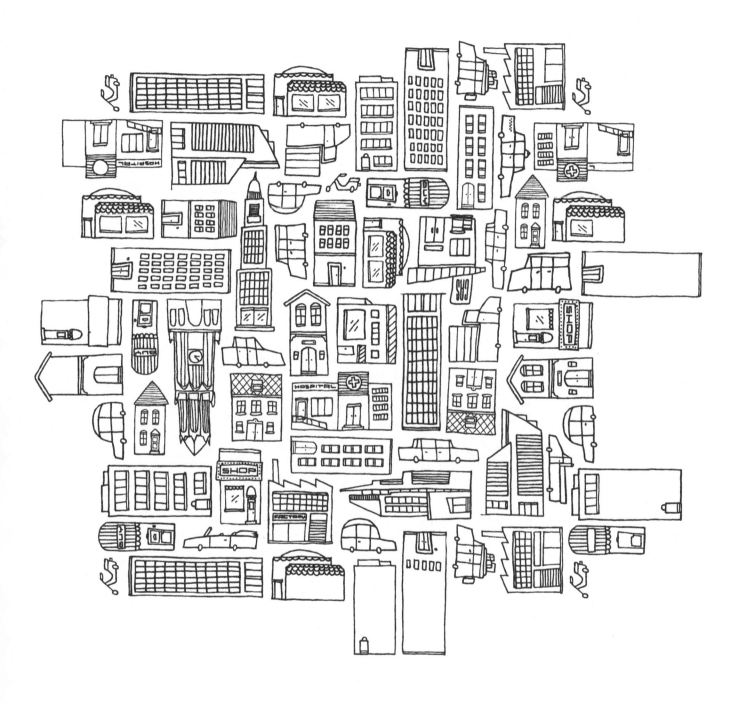

"The mundaneness of place is an
illusion. Any place can give birth to
the kingdom of G-d."
Jordan Peterson

"Imagine what your life could be like if you organized the smallest element to the largest element."
Jordan Peterson

"The star that glitters in the night is the transcendent ideal that makes itself manifest to you . . . if you listen quietly."
Jordan Peterson

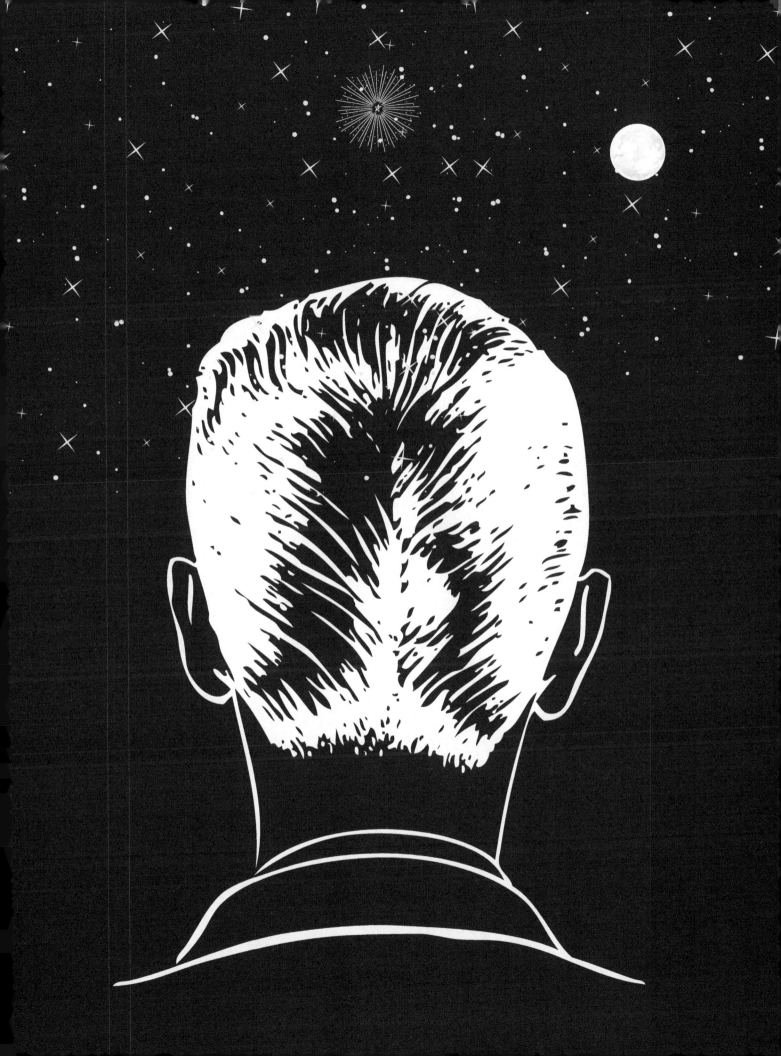

"We fall captive to the herd animal if we cannot reach the individual divinity in ourselves."
Carl Jung

"MAKE YOUR OWN BIBLE. SELECT AND COLLECT ALL THE WORDS AND SENTENCES THAT IN ALL YOUR READINGS HAVE BEEN TO YOU LIKE THE BLAST OF A TRUMPET." RALPH WALDO EMERSON

Jordan Peterson said: truth ". . . snaps things together. . . . You have a nature, and when you feel that nature articulated, it's like the act of snapping the puzzle pieces together." For those of us who read and listen to Jordan Peterson, we know exactly what he's talking about. He has a knack for articulating concepts with such poignancy, with such insight . . . You hear the click!

I'm hoping that this introduction to some of the poignant insights of Dr. Jordan Peterson will prompt you to tune in to his YouTube channel and go back for more! If you do, you will find many gems there! And I encourage you to take notes. Write down the ones that resonate for you. Keep them near at hand. Many of us have done exactly that. So I've created some pages for your collection and I'm going to start you off. A few more by Dr. Jordan Peterson:

"You have all of these miserable people with problems you can't imagine to believe...and look, the lights are on."

"It isn't precisely that people will fight for what they believe. They will fight, instead, to maintain the match between what they believe, what they expect, and what they desire."

Don't tell yourself, "I shouldn't need to do that to motivate myself." What do you know about yourself? You are, on the one hand, the most complex thing in the entire universe, and on the other, someone who can't even set the clock on your microwave. Don't overestimate your self-knowledge.

The world is a forum for sharing and trading, not a treasurer-house for the plundering. To give us to do what you can to make things better. The good in people will respond to that, and support it, and imitated, and multiply it, and return it, and foster it, so that everything improves and moves forward.

"You are obligated not to associate with people who are trying to damage the structure of being."

Quotes & Notes

Quotes & Notes

Lobster University Press

Jordan Peterson's *Maps of Meaning: The Architecture of Belief* and the opus of his work, more generally, is vast in scope and complex in nature. I have launched Lobster University Press, named tongue in cheek, for sure, but also with a vision in mind. Peterson relays many ideas that we can unpack, ideas that can help us scale the hierarchy or get a tougher shell to endure life's hardships; maybe even indirectly raise the production of serotonin!

The books published within this series will address specific themes covered by Peterson in his books and lectures. These materials are designed to help readers better integrate Peterson's ideas and to expand readers' 'map of meaning' and tweak that most important of abilities: the capacity to "turn chaos into habitable order!"

An Illustrated Guide for Using Jordan Peterson's Insights on Divinity & the Map of Meaning to Sort Yourself Out

According to Dr. Jordan Peterson, secular society has overlooked the psychological importance of Divinity, failing to understand the template it provides that helps us flourish. If Peterson is right, we need to review what classic texts tell us about the intricate and specific structure of the G-dhead. Lo and behold, that exact structure pervades creation as a whole, serving as DNA that undergirds the physical world, the human body, the contours of the psyche and more.

In this book, Annette Poizner first explores Peterson's insights about Divinity, then traces the imprint of Divinity on creation. Exploring the nooks and crannies of our world - surveying diverse areas including graphic design, cultural norms, marketing practices, handedness and more - allows us to see unity, the watermark of Divinity, at the root of creation. As we explore the central pattern at play, we delve into a visual adventure: learning the structure of Divinity by - believe it or not - analyzing the handwriting of public figures.

Poizner introduces Clinical Graphology, a bona fide European technique for assessing personality, to illustrate how the template of Divinity is our first and only nature. Learning about Oprah, Streisand, Deepak Chopra and others, you will learn about yourself! Explore the profound truths about self and soul that flow each time you pick up a pen . . . en route to our ultimate destination, not to know the rich and famous, but to know G-d and Self.

In a work 15 years in the making, Poizner weaves together the ideas of Jordan Peterson, Jewish Mysticism, Chinese medical theory, Jungian psychology, and 30 years of clinical experience, to survey the interior of our world from a most unique vantage point.

This Way Up: A Faith-Based Introduction to Jordan Peterson's 'Maps of Meaning'

'Jordan Peterson's books are selling furiously, widely cited in the media and part of an ongoing conversation. This book addresses why those in the faith-based communities should familiarize themselves with this work. Annette Poizner argues that Peterson's work is awakening the hearts and minds of a generation, prompting an army of young people to question the premises of secularism and ponder the tenets of faith. In this *zeitgeist*, clergy and laypeople are better equipped to address the needs of young people walking through their doors if they understand the worldview Peterson is advancing. This book is designed to summarize some of Peterson's important concepts including his ideas about the nature of reality and its constituent aspects, the structure of the mind, and the psychological necessity of the God ideal. These ideas will be presented through the lens of faith, referring to teachings which are drawn from a detailed study of the text of Genesis, so believers of monotheistic religions can explore how Peterson's concepts can be personally useful to readers of various faiths and denominations.

In Good Standing: Using Jordan Peterson's Insights on the Structure of Self to Sort Yourself Out

Your self has a structure, indirectly alluded to by Dr. Jordan Peterson each time he counsels you to live in alignment, whenever he urges you to stand with your shoulders back and every time he urges you to notice where you're aiming. Even the English 'Personal Pronoun I' alludes to that structure. Look carefully. Back 8 words. See it? It's a straight line.

Annette Poizner asserts that the archetype of the line, unpacked, delivers a myriad of lessons which can be applied to master the living of life. She will introduce the three-step pattern that underpins reality, expressed in hormonal patterns and stoplights, revealed in classic myths and modern-day acronyms, applied in building structures and hair braiding techniques. In all these, we find a trinity that sits at the root of creation, one referred to in the day-to-day vernacular as "beginning, middle and end," so naming the three points on a straight line. Watch as the contours of reality come into focus, bringing an awareness of a structure that pervades creation . . . and, more importantly, yourself.

Poizner, a seasoned clinician, doctoral level practitioner and certified graphologist, will pepper this presentation with references from the Hebrew Bible, other sources and with handwritings of prominent public figures! Turns out that we dance with the straight line each time we pick up a pen! We will meet the line in all its manifestations and befriend the archetype that grows us up, helps us stand tall, aims us forward and culminates, ideally, in a singular ego identity. We will come to see that each lie is nothing but a line with a missing piece and will understand that we spell our best success when we embrace the G-d-given archetype and, in so doing, actualize our Divine birthright. We have, after all, been lovingly made in the image of the One, the Only.

With a book designed to change your map of meaning and your perspective of life, you can take Peterson's ideas to the next level. Insights advanced by Rabbi Dr. Akiva Tatz, a Talmudic sage whose scope and intellect matches that of Peterson, will be harnessed by your guide, an author whose psychotherapy practice of 30 years compels a practical vision of what readers need to know to make meaningful and lasting life changes.

From Chaos to Order: A Guide to Jordan Peterson's Worldview

Struggling to decipher Jordan Peterson's core worldview when you listen on YouTube? Finding that his mosaic style, fascinating tangents and detours into the mythic realm make him hard to follow? Or maybe you're wondering what the fuss is about and would like a concise introduction to Jordan Peterson's mentality, particularly as it relates to the task of sorting yourself out?

In this book, a seasoned therapist takes you on a tour of Peterson's central ideas. In a clear, linear presentation, Annette Poizner presents Peterson's premises about reality and the specific ways we perceive and organize that reality. She introduces his ideas regarding the map of meaning, outlines his take on how and why our life maps are easily corrupted and follows with his premises about the psychological necessity of the God ideal, tracing the sequelae when that ideal is absent, as it is in secular society. Finally, Poizner renders Peterson's map of the life space. We come to see how his rules help readers thrive in reality, given the contours of reality that he discusses. Prepare to see life from a unique, surprising and relevant vantage point.

In providing the scaffolding of Peterson's core arguments, Poizner gifts readers with a big picture that will help them when they read or listen to Peterson, facilitating better comprehens-

-ion and alleviating some of the inevitable review normally required when working through his material. At the same time, this work bridges material from his two bestselling books, his Biblical lecture series and his University of Toronto courses, depicting overarching themes that emerge across platforms and presenting those clinical insights that have implications for contemporary life. Readers gain a lens through which they can consider their own personal process and are given reflection points that they can use to explore the personal relevance of ideas discussed. Please note: Four chapters from the initial book published by Lobster University Press, *A Practical Summary & Workbook for Using Jordan Peterson's Insights to Sort Yourself Out*, have been reprinted in this volume.

Beyond Chaos: Wrestling with Jordan Peterson's Notion of the Feminine

Thousands report that Jordan Peterson's insights have helped them achieve life-altering change. Yet, by Peterson's own admission, the lion's share of his followers are male. Are there jewels in his opus which could be accessed by women? Annette Poizner says there are, but first this group needs to better understand what Peterson is actually saying about the feminine. Materials needs to be prepared which will speak to the female sensibility and help dismantle the resistance that prevents some women from approaching Peterson's work.

Does Peterson's talk of 'chaos' as feminine trigger you? Do you disagree with many of his political positions? Poizner asserts that approaching his material with a will to understand yields rewards: readers can benefit from insights, ideas that usefully deviate from the usual societal narrative, while maintaining the license to reject those (political or otherwise) that don't jibe for any given woman. She asserts that women can benefit from the materials that Peterson has generously shared online, leveraging insights to achieve significant personal change and delving into constructs of masculine and feminine that are as old as antiquity.

Poizner, a therapist/social worker, brings unique credentials to the task of introducing Peterson's opus specifically to those women who have, to date, stood in opposition. Born in the 60's, Poizner grew up an avid feminist and remains committed to progress for women. Her clinical work, steeped in Chinese medical theory, the wisdom of the ancient Kabbalah and the psychology of Carl Jung, equips her to perform a rich and detailed rendering of Yin and Yang, masculine and feminine, towards the end of unpacking Peterson's frame in a way that brings the teachings to life.

Poizner, who herself differs with Peterson on a range of issues, is working to provide a bridge for women who need help getting over the hump: helping them understand where Peterson has been vilified and misquoted, where he advances clinical insight that can be used to make life better and where they can easily agree to disagree with him. In terms of the latter, in so doing women can deliciously host the paradox of life, itself; the paradox that the masculine and feminine polarities are, more than anything else, here to teach us; the paradox, that represents the central task of life, what we are here to learn.

Finding One Self: A Teenager's Guide for Using Jordan Peterson's Rules to Sort Yourself Out

Countless young men have been helped by the ideas of Canadian psychologist Jordan Peterson. The question remains: does this psychologist's opus of work have something to offer young women in their teens?

Clinical Social Worker & Therapist Annette Poizner suggests it does: young women will be fascinated to learn about the map of meaning that they harbor within, a map that the unconscious mind builds to manage chaos, an inherent part of reality. In this book, readers access a peek into the galaxy of Jordan Peterson, learning rules and ideas that they can use to architect their best self, enhance self-image and use as an anchor, in the face of normlessness.

Drawing on decades of clinical experience, Poizner speaks directly to young women, tailoring the rules to a reality heavy on electronics, light on consensus. Short chapters provide useable soundbites. Readers walk away with strategies to make changes and get a personalized introduction to Dr. Peterson's work, designed for those new to some ideas that have taken the world by storm!

Unlocking Hidden Meaning in Signatures: An Illustrated Guide to Symbol & Self

"The way you write, draw, dream, joke or remember embodies more information than you know."

Dr. Jordan Peterson

"You have a pattern of behavior that characterizes you "

Dr. Jordan Peterson

"He that has eyes to see and ears to hear may convince himself that no mortal can keep a secret. If his lips are silent, he chatters with his fingertips; betrayal oozes out of him at every pore."

Sigmund Freud

Though a common phrase in the business vernacular, clinician Annette Poizner suggests that those familiar words – sign here – point to a hidden truth: embedded within any given signature are signs – symbols – that potentially reveal personality style, interests or behavioral patterns of the writer. Right here, before our eyes, is information that can reveal personality and orientation, the writer's 'personal brand'. Readers can access tentative insights which can better help them understand themselves and others, all as near as the stroke of a pen.

Examining the signatures of well-known celebrities, you will be looking over the shoulder of an experienced graphologist and psychotherapist. Explore the inner dynamics revealed - often quite overtly albeit undetected by those without training - when a person provides a signature, the moniker that each person cultivates to express self and soul. Dabble in the intriguing world of projective personality assessment which has clinicians observing and evaluating every day

behaviors, like handwriting, drawing, telling stories or remembering jokes, all of which provide a medium for self-expression. A trained observer will unpack layers of information. Get to know Justin Trudeau, Barbra Streisand, Justin Bieber, Donald Trump, Katie Couric amongst many others on the basis of signatures, en route to getting a better understanding of the human condition as it plays out in each one of us.

Getting Sorted, Lobster Style: Why (and How) You Can Use Jordan Peterson's Insights to Make Life Better

You've heard about Dr. Jordan Peterson. You know people who hate him. Others, though, seem to be using his ideas to make life changes. Maybe you are wondering how to think about this psychologist and his ideas.

Author and Therapist Annette Poizner, a clinical social worker, has prepared a series of articles for those contemplating a deeper look at this opus of work. She makes the case for exploring Peterson's talks and books, noting the license to work with some of his notions and reject others, and introduces venues for discussing and debating his worldview with others who are contemplating his ideas. Poizner suggests that some people may be able to architect important personal changes on the strength of what they learn from Peterson, without the counsel and expense involved in seeing an individual therapist.

This book is designed to provide an entry point for the curious, providing the rationale for probing this work further despite the hot button issues that have tangentially been related to Peterson's line of thinking.

This Way Up: A Faith-Based Introduction to Jordan Peterson's 'Maps of Meaning'

Can faith help us cope with the difficult times ahead? This book introduces Jordan Peterson's insights about the importance of Divinity in our lives and notes that Peterson's work is awakening the hearts and minds of a generation, prompting an army of young people to question the premises of secularism and ponder the tenets of faith.

This book is designed to summarize some of Peterson's important concepts including his ideas about the nature of reality and its constituent aspects, the structure of the mind, and the psychological necessity of the G-d ideal. These ideas will be presented through the lens of faith, referring to teachings which are drawn from a detailed study of the text of Genesis. Believers of monotheistic religions can explore how Peterson's concepts can be personally useful to readers of various backgrounds and denominations. In a book designed for both clergy and laypeople, both groups can be better facilitated with a fuller understanding of those ideas that are shaping a generation.

Lobster Tales: Stories of Lives Transformed by the Work of Jordan Peterson

The name Jordan Peterson evokes strong responses: rave reviews from many, upset from others troubled by political views which touch sensitive nerves.

Undecided readers, those trying to make sense of the man and his work, would do well to explore some of the stories of those who looked beyond the media storm to access ideas that have helped them. In this book, therapist Annette Poizner, a clinical social worker, documents tales of transformation, tracking the stories of people who used Peterson's ideas to architect change. Read about how Peterson's opus has been redemptive, helping some overcome severe addictions, helping a white supremacist see the error of his ways, a formerly homeless man now in graduate school, who credits that transformation to Peterson's opus.Stranger than fiction, these stories will compel you to look and look again at work that might help you reach your goals. What have you got to lose? This living document will continue to be updated over time, as more stories come to light, helping us all understand the power and potential embedded in Peterson's nuanced worldview and philosophy.

Annette Poizner, MSW, Ed.D., RSW, is a Toronto-based clinical social worker in private practice who has studied much of the work of Dr. Jordan B. Peterson. She has a Master's Degree in Social Work from Columbia University of New York and a Doctorate of Education, specializing in Counseling Psychology, granted by the University of Toronto. Her work has garnered extensive media attention. Bringing techniques that are mainstream in parts of Europe and Israel, her work has been featured in dailies across Canada, in trade magazines across North America and showcased at academic and clinical conferences. She served as a senior consultant at the 2016 TED Talks in British Columbia.

She is the author of "Clinical Graphology: An Interpretive Manual for Mental Health Practitioners," published by Charles C Thomas Publishers, an academic publishing house, She has launched Lobster University Press, written many volumes about the work of Dr. Jordan Peterson and authored books on other topics, as well, most of which can be accessed via her website: ap.annettepoizner.com.

Books By Dr. Jordan Peterson

Peterson, Jordan (1999) *Maps of Meaning: The Architecture of Belief.* New York: Routledge..

Peterson, Jordan (2018). *The 12 Rules for Life: The Architecture of Belief.* Toronto, Canada: Random House Canada.

Peterson, Jordan (2021). *Beyond Order: 12 More Rules or Life.* Toronto, Canada: Portfolio.

For more information about the work of Jordan Peterson, please visit www.jordanpeterson.com.

For discussion about the work of Jordan Peterson please visit related groups on Facebook.

THE MOON IN THE MAN

A Carl Jung Coloring Book
for Self-Exploration

By Annette Poizner, MSW.

INNER NATURE

*A Carl Jung Coloring Book
for Self-Exploration*

By Annette Poizner, MSW, Ed.D., RSW

Made in the USA
Coppell, TX
06 October 2022